The Christma Cavalier

A pantomime

Richard Lloyd

Samuel French – London
New York – Sydney – Toronto – Hollywood

TO MANDY

THE CHRISTMAS CAVALIER

First performed on Saturday, 10th December, 1988, by
Theatre Workshop, Coulsdon, with the following cast:

Nicholas Grimnasty	Mike Brown
Matthew Smallpiece	Lee Wilkinson
Obadiah Stupid	Tim Young
Nathaniel Stupid	Simeon Dawes
Dame Dumplings	Chris Argles
Emma Sweetly	Lisa King
Sir Daniel Dash	Penny Simeone
Peter Farthing	Richard Lloyd
Bottom	Pete Gregory
The Three Witches	Wendy Cole
	Lesley Argles
	Christine Blake
Village Children	Martin Cole
	Kimberley Argles
	Bryony Eida
	Dawn Lock
	Nichola Newton
	Maria New
	Wendy New
	Luke Argles
	Ian Shaw
	John Shaw
Father Christmas	Paul M. Ford

Directed by Richard Lloyd
Musical Director Mark Taylor

SYNOPSIS OF SCENES

CHARACTERS

Nicholas Grimnasty, the Witchfinder General
Matthew Smallpiece, his assistant
Obadiah Stupid, a Roundhead Trooper
Nathaniel Stupid, also a Roundhead Trooper
Dame Dumplings, an outrageous old woman
Emma Sweetly, her niece
Peter Farthing, a pedlar
Bottom, a performing bear
Sir Daniel Dash, a bold and gallant cavalier
Village Children, odious brats
The Three Crones/Witches, vile snaggle-toothed hags

MUSIC

The choice of songs, dances etc is left to individual Directors, but please read the note printed below issued by the Performing Right Society, very carefully. A licence issued by Samuel French Ltd to perform this play does NOT include permission to use any copyright music in the performance. The notice printed below on behalf of the Performing Right Society should be carefully read.

The following statement concerning the use of music is printed here on behalf of the Performing Right Society Ltd, by whom it was supplied

The permission of the owner of the performing right in copyright music must be obtained before any public performance may be given, whether in conjunction with a play or sketch or otherwise, and this permission is just as necessary for amateur performances as for professional. The majority of copyright musical works (other than oratorios, musical plays and similar dramatico-musical works) are controlled in the British Commonwealth by the PERFORMING RIGHT SOCIETY LTD, 29–33 BERNERS STREET, LONDON W1P 4AA.

The society's practice is to issue licences authorizing the use of its repertoire to the proprietors of premises at which music is publicly performed, or, alternatively, to the organizers of musical entertainments, but the Society does not require payment of fees by performers as such. Producers or promoters of plays sketches, etc., at which music is to be performed, during or after the play or sketch, should ascertain whether the premises at which their performances are to be given are covered by a licence issued by the Society, and if they are not, should make application to the Society for particulars as to the fee payable.

NOTES ON CHARACTERIZATION

Although *The Christmas Cavalier* is a new story, all the characters in the play fit into the framework of traditional pantomime. They should be portrayed as larger than life, and their qualities (good or bad) exaggerated. Remember, pantomime characters are not real people, but grotesque caricatures.

Nicholas Grimnasty, the Witchfinder General. Grimnasty is the archetypal pantomime villain, possessed of all the worst characteristics of the breed. He is cruel, overbearing, and downright unpleasant in every respect! Grimnasty must be played with unremitting melodrama, and at maximum volume!

Matthew Smallpiece, the Witchfinder's Assistant. Smallpiece is the quintessential sidekick. Sneaky and mean-spirited, he goes in terror of his master—and takes it out on everybody else! Although he is the butt of many jokes, Smallpiece's evil is of a more refined variety, and he should be played as the proverbial "nasty piece of work".

Dame Dumplings. Dame Dumplings is overweight, coarse, loud and objectionable. In fact, all that a pantomime Dame should be! She is also colourful, resilient and funny—qualities which endear her to us and the audience . . .

Emma Sweetly. Dame Dumpling's niece displays all the best characteristics of a principal girl. She is pretty, kind and loving. She is also vivacious, and with a touch of steel perhaps not always found in such a role. For Emma has another side to her character, a side which is revealed once she has fallen under Grimnasty's evil spell. . .

Sir Daniel Dash, the Christmas Cavalier. Nor is this bold and gallant cavalier struck from quite the same mould as other principal boys. True, he is swashbuckling and brave, with a resplendent uniform and boyish good looks. But he lacks one commodity—a sense of humour—being the one truly "straight" character in the show. He takes everything very seriously, with stiff upper lip, and a peremptory manner. He should be admired, rather than liked.

Nathaniel and Obadiah Stupid. These two Roundhead troopers fulfill the traditional role of "Broker's Men". They are engaging idiots, who start out as unwilling henchmen of the villain, but turn up trumps in the end. They should be physically contrasting—one short and fat, the other tall and thin—and played strictly for laughs. Obadiah is marginally the more stupid of the pair, and should possess more than a hint of pathos.

Peter Farthing. Although only a small role, Peter Farthing is pivotal to the plot. He is an earthy, elemental character, and should remind us of a sort of "Jack in the Green", appearing at once simple and wise. For there is more to Peter Farthing than meets the eye . . .

The Three Crones/Witches. These three are a conglomerate of all the corniest witches to have trodden stage and screen. They should be played with absolute conviction, and completely over the top!

Bottom. A bear, as they say, of very little brain. (But a lovely disposition.)

Village Children. Who should be the naughtiest, rudest, most excitable children ever to poke fun at a Dame!

There is no separate adult chorus, although if bodies are available, they could certainly be usefully incorporated as villagers, soldiers, and the like.

Long, long ago, in the land of England, there was a war between the King and his Parliament.

The Parliament won the war—and the King lost his head.

Power fell to the hands of an austere puritan named Cromwell, who, despising all revelry and jollity as frivolous and ungodly, determined to abolish the great festival of Christmas.

So it was, that he sent agents out into the villages and countryside, to stamp out Christmas wherever it was celebrated.

One such place was the village of . . .

ACT I

Overture

SCENE 1

The castle of the Witchfinder General

A dark and evil vault, hung with macabre banners. Mist drifts across a stage which is bare apart from a large throne on a dais C. Sinister music is heard. Thunder crashes and lightning flashes

Nathaniel and Obadiah Stupid enter. Two Roundhead troopers. They bang their halberds three times on the floor in unison

Nathaniel Silence in the name of the Lord Protector!

> *Smallpiece enters, garbed in evil cape and ludicrously outsized Puritan hat. He laughs wickedly and sits on the throne*

Smallpiece Silence for the Witchfinder General!

> *The Witchfinder General enters to sinister chords. He also wears an evil cape and Puritan hat. He laughs villainously*

Smallpiece quickly vacates the throne

Witchfinder Ha ha ha ha! I, Nicholas Grimnasty, Witchfinder General for the County of (*insert appropriate county*), in this year of our Lord, sixteen hundred and fifty, hereby declare, in the name of Oliver Cromwell, Lord Protector of England, that Christmas is ABOLISHED! Ha ha ha ha!!!

Audience participation

> This decree is final! There will be no more singing of carols or giving of presents, no more parties, nor feasting and drinking. In fact—no more enjoying yourselves at all!

Audience participation

> Silence you miserable peasants, or I'll have you all locked up in the stocks!

Audience participation

> Oh yes I will! (*Etc.*) Furthermore, I am here on business. Witchfinding business. Anyone offering information regarding the whereabouts of witches, will be richly rewarded. So, who has anything they'd like to tell me?

Audience participation

Bah! You village idiots! I do not need your pathetic help anyway! I shall catch my own witches. I am an expert at catching witches. Smallpiece!

Nathaniel and Obadiah examine their breeches ostentatiously. They look at each other. Nathaniel nudges Smallpiece, who is staring glumly at his feet

Smallpiece (*servilely*) Yes, Master?
Witchfinder How many guilty witches have I convicted this year?
Smallpiece (*promptly*) None, M'Lud.
Witchfinder What?!!
Smallpiece Well they weren't actually guilty if you remember, M'Lud. We framed most of them and——
Witchfinder SILENCE YOU IMBECILE!!! I will tell you how many witches I have had burned at the stake this year—ninety-nine! And I intend to make it one hundred by Christmas! Ha ha ha ha!!!

Audience participation

And do you know how I find them?

Audience participation

Tell them how I find them, Smallpiece.
Smallpiece (*sturdily*) You smell, M'Lud.
Witchfinder What?!
Smallpiece You smell, M'Lud. You sniff 'em out!
Witchfinder Yes! Ha ha! I sniff them out. I winkle them out of their holes and whisk them off to my castle. After a few days in the dungeons, they can't wait to confess!

Audience participation

And now, I shall apply the same technique to anyone suspected of enjoying themselves at Christmas. Especially the kiddies!! Ha ha ha!!

Audience participation

Song (Witchfinder)

Smallpiece! Which village are we visiting next?
Smallpiece Er . . . (*insert local town*), M'Lud.
Witchfinder Not that place with all the Chinese take-aways? (*Or other local joke*)
Smallpiece That's it, M'Lud.
Witchfinder Bah! What a dump!

Audience participation
Still I'm sure we'll be able to find a witch or two there! Lead on, we're all going to have a really miserable Christmas! Ha ha ha ha!!

All exit to audience participation

SCENE 2

Ye Olde Village of (local town)

A rustic winter setting. A number of snow-laden cottages

A string of snugly-wrapped children file on. They are singing the carol "Silent Night" in German. Halting before the door of a particularly delapidated dwelling, a small, rather badly behaved boy steps up and raps on the door

There is a crashing and banging from within, then a voice

Dame (*off*) All right, all right, I'm coming! I'm just stuffing a tart!

There are more crashes, the front door flies open, and Dame Dumplings bowls out

Oh look everybody! How sweet! The dear little children of the village out singing carols.

Boy (*holding out his cap*) And collectin' money.

Dame Of course dear. How terribly traditional. (*Her expression changes*) Hoppit!

All Go on, Dame Dumplings, give us a donation, please. (*They resume their carol*)

"Stille Nacht, heilige Nacht ..."

Dame Oi! Hold on a minute. Don't you lot know any English carols?

All Yes.

Dame Well here's a groat for your trouble. Go and sing one somewhere else. (*She drops a tiny coin into the boy's cap*)

Boy (*in disbelief*) Only a groat!

Dame Very observant dear, you're obviously a cub.

Girl Go on, Dame Dumplings, you can spare more than a groat ... it is Christmas.

Dame That's as maybe dear, but I've got a lot of outgoings I have ... (*she gestures to her premises*) ... I've got all this to support!

Boy (*prodding her stomach*) All this to support more like!

Dame Oooh!

Girl Yes, go on, Dame Dumplings. Lay off the stout for a few days and you could spare us a few more pence!

Dame (*outraged*) Stout! I don't know what you mean! What a sauce!

She goes inside and slams the front door

Boy Cor! What a rotten meanie!

Girl (*loudly*) YES, SHE'S A ROTTEN MEANIE!

There is no reaction

Boy (*loudly*) MY DAD'S ALWAYS SAID SHE WAS A ROTTEN MEANIE!

Still no reaction

Girl (*conspiratorially*) My dad says she's a witch!

The door flies open and Dame Dumplings rushes out

Dame WHAT?!!
Girl My Dad says you're a witch.
Dame (*grabbing her by the ear*) Now you shouldn't go around saying that sort of thing. That could land me in a lot of serious trouble that could!
Girl (*innocently*) Really?
Dame Yes really!

The boy extends his cap again

Oh all right! Here's your money, you beastly little reptiles. Now sling yer hook!

She shoos them away with her broom

Talk about extortion! I mean to say! Witch indeed! Ha! . . . I'm just a wise woman that's all. The Wise Woman of (*local town*) they call me round here.
Boy (*from a safe distance*) No they don't. They call you Fatso Wobblebottom!
Dame Now look here . . .
Girl Or, the Old Hag at Number Twenty-Seven!
Dame Oooh! You little horrors! Just you wait . . .

She chases the children round in circles, swiping at them with her broom. Suddenly, a bell is heard ringing, off

What's that? Can't be the interval already can it? (*To the audience*) Nobody's that lucky!

A voice is heard off

Peter   (*off; chanting*) Have you got any pots or pans or kettles to fettle?
                  Me rivets are made of the very best metal!
Children (*excitedly*) It's Peter Farthing the Pedlar!

A scruffy individual in outlandish garb enters. He is loaded with bags and bundles of wares

HURRAY!! (*They run to surround the newcomer*) Peter! Peter Farthing!
Peter Hallo children! (*He hands out some sweets*)

The children exit chattering and laughing

Dame (*aside*) Blimey! Peter Farthing? Should call himself Peter American Express, the prices he charges! (*Calling*) Oi! Pedlar! On yer bike! (*To the audience*) Pedlar—on yer bike—geddit?! Oh, suit yourself!
Peter Hallo Dame Dumplings. Here, have you seen my Bottom recently?
Dame (*shocked*) What?!
Peter Have you seen me dancing bear?
Dame I 'aven't seen you dancing at all, mate, let alone . . . well, you know

Peter I can't find him anywhere. I only went off for a moment and left me bear behind. When I came back——

Dame (*interrupting*) I do wish you'd stop going on about that!

Peter What?

Dame Your bare behind! Your bottom! The very idea makes me feel quite nauseating.

Peter No, no. You don't understand.

Dame That's nothing new . . .

Peter Dame Dumplings, surely you remember me performing bear?

Dame Oooooh!!! It gets worse! You rude man! I remember no such thing! Go on, hoppit! (*She belabours him with her broom*) Sling yer hook! (*She chases him off*)

Peter exits

Really! I don't know what things are coming to around here. I feel all of a do-dither now! Oooh the palpitations!

A voice is heard off, singing sweetly

Oh, that'll be my dear little niece Emma. Emma Sweetly . . . She's so sweet she could give you tooth decay . . . She lives with me, you know . . .

Emma enters carrying flowers, singing sweetly

Emma Hallo Auntie.

Dame Hallo dear, where have you been then? Gathering pretty flowers in the forest?

Emma (*puzzled*) No. The florists.

Dame Oh.

Emma But I did go for a walk in the forest . . .

Dame Did you? Oh that's nice my little sugarplum . . .

Emma (*wistfully*) Yes . . . I met a man . . .

Dame (*suspiciously*) Really?

Emma (*more wistfully*) Yes. A bold and gallant cavalier of the King . . .

Dame (*clamping a hand over Emma's mouth*) SHHHH!!! You'll get us into trouble you will, talking about cavaliers and kings like they was still in fashion!

Emma He was disguised as a woodman . . .

Dame Could have been worse, he could have been disguised as the (*insert notorious local pub*).

Emma But I knew he was a gallant cavalier.

Dame Oh yus? And how may I ask?

Emma He showed me his credentials.

Dame Really! And how did you know they were authentic?

Emma Er . . . he told me.

Dame I see. And I suppose he'd just finished helping Prince Charles to escape to France, had he?

Emma Er . . . yes. How did you know?

Dame And I daresay he thought that deserved a little kiss, did he?

Emma Well . . . er . . .

Dame I see.

Emma Oh but Auntie, he was devastatingly handsome, and I'm sure he really was a cavalier!

Dame Yes, well, if he was, we're well rid of him. He'd only cause trouble. (*She starts to sweep*)

Emma I was so sad when we parted, but then I thought—I'll see him again——

Dame (*patronizingly*) Yes dear, of course you will.

Emma —when he comes here.

Dame (*spluttering*) What do you mean "when he comes here", he's not coming here!

Emma Oh but he is. I invited him.

Dame (*grabbing Emma by the scruff of the neck*) No he ruddy well isn't! It'll mean all sorts of trouble! You get along inside, my girl. I'll talk to you later!

Emma But Auntie ...

Dame No buts! In you go! (*She shows Emma into the cottage*)

Emma exits into the cottage

I don't know, these young girls today have got no idea. Now when I was a girl ...

Sir Daniel Dash, a bold and gallant cavalier, enters, tokenly disguised as a woodcutter

Sir Daniel (*peremptorily*) Old woman!

Dame (*looking around*) Where?!

Sir Daniel Yes, you! You must be Dame Pudding.

Dame (*coldly*) Dumplings.

Sir Daniel Er ... quite so. Now, listen here, my good woman, I am looking for the house of Emma Sweetly.

Dame Oh yes? And who might you be?

Sir Daniel I am ... er ... well, a humble woodcutter ...

Dame Well you're in the wrong pantomime then, mate. You want *Little Red Riding Hood*! (*She turns to leave*)

Sir Daniel Wait! Very well, I am—(*He throws back his cloak impressively*)—Sir Daniel Dash, a cavalier of the King!

Dame (*flatly*) King's dead. They cut 'is 'ead orf.

Sir Daniel (*irritated*) The LATE King. I have recently returned from helping Prince Charles escape to France and——

Dame (*interrupting*) Yes, yes, all right. You can spare me all the old polish mate.

Sir Daniel Madam! I am a Cornet in the King's Army!

Dame (*aside*) A cornet? Blimey! Looks more like a choc ice, doesn't he ... Ooh look, it's the scowling cavalier!

Sir Daniel I can prove that I am who I say I am.

Dame (*uncomprehendingly*) Eh?

Sir Daniel I can prove my identity!

Dame Oh yus? And how may I be so bold as to ask?

Sir Daniel (*reverently*) I have in my keeping, the King's signet ring. I hold it for the Prince, until he returns to claim his father's throne! (*He shows her the ring*)

Dame Oooer! It looks like the real thing! The Great Seal of Olde England! Well blow me! He is a real Cavalier. Ooh sir, Your Lordship, how can I ever apologize for having doubted you? If there is any way in which I can possibly be of any assistance ...

Sir Daniel Well, actually I——

Dame (*quickly*) No you can't stay here!

Sir Daniel Why not?

Dame (*conspiratorially*) It would be dangerous.

Sir Daniel (*slapping his thigh*) Ha! Danger! My old adversary, I'm well used to his company!

Dame (*briskly*) Yes, but I'm not, so you'll have to shove off I'm afraid.

Sir Daniel Dame Dumplings, I need shelter for but a few days. If you are a loyal and true subject of the Crown, you cannot deny me. You must give me succour!

Dame Well I don't know about that ...

Sir Daniel (*sternly*) It is your duty!

Dame Oh all right, all right! Don't go on about it. You can stay. But only for a few days. And only if you promise to keep a low profile.

Sir Daniel Very well, you have my word, madam.

Dame Right then.

Sir Daniel Agreed.

Dame Fine.

They shake hands

Sir Daniel (*bellowing*) EMMA! EMMA!

Dame (*depressed*) So much for the low profile ...

Emma runs out of the cottage

Emma Oh Daniel! Daniel, you're here!

Sir Daniel Yes! And your aunt says I may stay——

Dame For a few days.

Emma Oh Daniel!

Sir Daniel Oh Emma!

They clasp hands and gaze lovingly into each other's eyes

Dame (*hastily moving between them and breaking them up with her broom*) Oh no! We'll have none of that! You, my girl, can go and buy some new decorations for the Village Christmas Party ... and collect Mistress Turnip's mince pies on the way back, will you? She's baked some specially.

Emma exits, gazing lingeringly at Daniel

Sir Daniel (*once she has gone*) What shall I do?

Dame Well you're supposed to be a woodcutter, aren't you? Go and cut some wood!

Sir Daniel Yes! (*Inspired*) Yes! I shall fell a Yule Log!

Sir Daniel exits

Dame (*calling after him*) Oh yes! That's right! Go and drag a dirty, great, muddy log into me nice, clean, front room! That's lovely that is! Blimey! What a country! Why we can't just have Christmas trees like the rest of Europe I don't know! Now then, where was I? Ooh! I nearly forgot! Me mince pies!

She rushes inside

SCENE 3

A forest

A number of sparse and gnarled trees. Eerie flickering lights can be seen, and ethereal silvan music heard

Three stooped and ancient Crones enter, gathering kindling

1st Crone How much wood have we collected, sisters?
2nd Crone (*holding up one very small twig*) All this.
1st Crone Is that it?
2nd Crone Look, I'm not a Fairy Godmother you know!
3rd Crone Not much of a forest really is it?
1st Crone
2nd Crone   (*together dismally*) No.
3rd Crone (*melodramatically*) Wait! A man is coming!
2nd Crone Ah! You have SEEN him!
3rd Crone No. I have HEARD him. Whistling jauntily.
2nd Crone *Jauntily*, no, don't think I know that one. How does it go?
1st Crone Shut up you old scragbags! I can see someone. Over there!
2nd Crone It is a woodman.
3rd Crone At least it's not (*another notorious local pub*)!
All Harrgh harrgh harrgh!

Sir Daniel enters, whistling jauntily, carrying a large log. He halts as he catches sight of the three old ladies

1st Crone Hail!
2nd Crone Hail!!
3rd Crone Hail!!!
Sir Daniel (*nonplussed*) Er ... Well met!
1st Crone Do what?
Sir Daniel Well met, Mistress Crookback!
1st Crone What's he going on about?
2nd Crone Blowed if I know. Why don't he talk proper English?
3rd Crone 'Ere! Ask him if he's got any wood!
1st Crone Oooh! Good idea! (*Feebly to Sir Daniel*) Kind sir, you wouldn't happen to have any small scraps of kindling about your person, to spare for three old ladies without fuel for a fire?

Sir Daniel Oh yes, certainly. Here, you can have this.

He tosses the log at the 1st Crone, who squeals and collapses under the weight

I don't think Dame Dumplings wanted it anyway.

3rd Crone One good turn deserves another. Is there any way in which we can repay your kindness?

Sir Daniel (*amused*) Good Lord! Shouldn't think so!

2nd Crone You may be surprised.

The Lights grow dim

We could tell you something about one very dear to you ...

Sir Daniel Really? Who?

2nd Crone Yourself!!!

Crones Harrgh harrgh harrgh!!!

Sir Daniel (*nervously*) What do you mean?

1st Crone Give me your hand.

Sir Daniel Why?

1st Crone So that I may read you of course!

Sir Daniel Look, I'm not a bally Mills and Boon novel you know!

2nd Crone We KNOW who you are!

Sir Daniel You do?

3rd Crone Your hand!

Sir Daniel (*extending his palm*) Oh very well!

1st Crone (*taking his hand and peering at it*) Aaaargh!!!

Sir Daniel What's the matter? What's wrong? What can you see?

1st Crone (*faintly*) It's clean ...

2nd Crone Clean!

3rd Crone Clean!!

Sir Daniel Well what's wrong with that?

1st Crone Well you're certainly not from around here!

2nd Crone What else do you see?

1st Crone Ah! I see a girlie!

2nd Crone A girlie!

3rd Crone A girlie!!

Sir Daniel (*feigning disinterest*) Er ... what sort of girlie exactly?

1st Crone Aiii! She is slender and fair!

2nd Crone (*peering at his palm*) And pretty. So very pretty.

3rd Crone With enormous big b——

1st Crone (*hastily*) Blue eyes!

Sir Daniel Ah! I know who that is. (*Getting interested*) What else can you see?

1st Crone I see a strange woman. You have only just met. She is grossly fat, and horrendously ugly!

Sir Daniel Of course! I know who that is as well!

1st Crone Who?

Sir Daniel It's you.

2nd Crone No, no, no! This woman is loud and common.

Sir Daniel Oh, in that case it must be Dame Dumplings.

1st Crone Aiii! Wait! I can see a man!
2nd Crone A fat man in a big black hat!
3rd Crone It is . . . it is . . . Aaaaargh!
1st Crone It is him! The one that seeks us!
3rd Crone We must flee sisters! Flee!

They start to hobble off

Sir Daniel I say! Hold on a moment! Who is this man?
1st Crone (*cryptically*) He is the one you must defeat!
Sir Daniel But how can I defeat him? I don't know who he is!
2nd Crone The girl! She is the key! Unlock the girl, and you will find the solution!
Sir Daniel But wait! Who are you? Are you the Wise Women?
1st Crone (*heavy sarcasm*) No, we're the (*local town*) Townswomen's Guild, and this is our annual picnic.

They exit

Sir Daniel Oh. (*Calling after them*) Goodbye! (*To the audience*) What mysterious old women. And I wonder who this fat feller in the big black hat is? Oh well. Better get back to the village I suppose. I might be in time to try one of Dame Dumplings' mince pies!

Sir Daniel exits

SCENE 4

The village

Nathaniel and Obadiah enter and proceed to nail up notices on the walls of the cottages. Nathaniel stands back to survey his handiwork

Nathaniel (*reading*) "No carol singing! By order of the Witchfinder General!"
Obadiah (*sitting on a tree-stump removing his helmet, and mopping his brow*) I'm sick of this, Nat!
Nathaniel What are you on about?
Obadiah All this Christmas business. I mean, I LIKE singing at Christmas. . . .
Nathaniel Well, you can still sing can't you? You just can't sing carols.
Obadiah (*glumly*) I know, but psalms don't have quite the same ring to them somehow . . . And what about Christmas Dinner? You know they've abolished mince pies and Christmas pud now, don't you?
Nathaniel Never mind. Just think how much weight you'll lose.
Obadiah That's all very well, but it's always the nice things they ban isn't it? I mean, they haven't abolished 'orrible, soggy brussel sprouts have they? Just lovely yummy, scrummy, Christmas pud! I'm fed up with all this gloom and misery! I mean, why do we have to do it, Nat?
Nathaniel (*importantly*) Because we're Roundheads, Obadiah.

Obadiah (*feeling his head foolishly*) Oh yes. I suppose we are really ...

Nathaniel Parliamentarians!

Obadiah Like Cecil Parkinson? (*Or other topical politician*)

Nathaniel No, not like Cecil Parkinson.

Obadiah Edwina Currie?!

Nathaniel NO! Nor Edwina Currie.

Obadiah Hey!

Nathaniel What?!

Obadiah I'm not a Roundhead, I'm not a Roundhead!

Nathaniel Of course you are.

Obadiah No, I'm not! I've got a bump just here see ... (*He invites Nathaniel to feel his head*)

Nathaniel Obadiah, you are without doubt the stupidest soldier in the entire army.

Obadiah Thank you, Nathaniel.

Nathaniel (*proudly*) We, Obadiah, are Ironsides!

Obadiah Are we?

Nathaniel Of course.

Obadiah (*prodding him in the ribs*) Where?!

Nathaniel grabs Obadiah and starts shaking him

Meanwhile, Dame Dumplings emerges from her cottage with a tray of hot mince pies. Her face lights up as she catches sight of the two squabbling soldiers

Dame (*to the audience*) Ooooh! Soldiers! Oh I do love a man in uniform. (*She adjusts her hair and her bosom*) Coooeee! Boys!

The two stop arguing and look round. They recoil in horror at the apparition confronting them

Song (Dame Dumplings)

During which Nathaniel and Obadiah perform a comic drill routine. At the end of the song ...

Nathaniel Er, yes? Miss?

Dame Hallo soldier! Fancy a nice hot tart?

Nathaniel Well ... er ... look, aren't you a bit on the old side for this sort of thing?

Dame Oooh! You saucy rogue! I'm certainly not too old! And I'm not a bit on the side either! I wasn't talking about that anyway. I meant these tarts. Luverly hot mince pies—(*proffering tray*)—fancy one?

Obadiah Cor! Yes!

Nathaniel (*stiffly*) Certainly not! Mince pies are against regulations—they're banned you know.

Dame Oh poppycock! Go on, have one.

Obadiah Yes go on. Let's have one?

Nathaniel NO!

Dame Oh well, suit yourself!

She sets the mince pies aside to cool, and starts sweeping her doorstep as Nathaniel and Obadiah resume their argument. After a few moments, she starts warbling a Christmas carol in a painful falsetto

Nathaniel Oi! You can't sing carols. They're banned as well.

Dame Oh go and boil your bottom!

Nathaniel (*lamely*) But you can't sing ...

Dame (*full of righteous indignation*) You can't come around here telling me what I can or can't sing! This is a free country you know ... As long as you aren't royalty that is ...

Nathaniel I'm not telling you WHAT you can't sing. I'm just pointing out THAT you can't sing. You sound like an ox stuck in a bog!

Dame (*hotly*) How dare you! I'll have you know I never sing when I'm stuck in the bog! (*Hurriedly*) Anyway, if you're such a great music critic—you give us a song!

Nathaniel No.

Dame Go on.

Nathaniel (*emphatically*) It isn't allowed.

Dame Garn! You just can't sing can you?!

Nathaniel Oh yes I can!

Dame (*encouraging the audience*) Oh no you can't!

Audience participation

Nathaniel Can!

Dame Can't!

Nathaniel Can!

Dame Can't!

Nathaniel Can!

Dame (*triumphantly catching him out*) Well go on then! (*To Obadiah*) Here, what's his favourite carol?

Nathaniel (*threateningly*) Shut up, Obadiah ...

Obadiah (*unhesitatingly*) *Away in a Manger.*

Dame Aaaah! Go on, sing it for us.

Nathaniel (*embarrassed*) I can't, not all on my own ...

Obadiah Here! What about getting some of these boys and girls to help?!

Dame Oooh yes! What a good idea! (*To the audience*) You'll help us sing a Christmas carol won't you?

Song

Audience participation song, followed by distribution of sweets and so on

There, that was fun wasn't it? Now then, where were we? Oooh! I haven't introduced myself have I? I'm Dame Dumplings, who are you?

Nathaniel Nathaniel Stupid.

Obadiah And Obadiah Stupid.

Both are treated to bone-crunching handshakes

Both At your service.

Dame Oh! You're brothers?

Both No.

Obadiah We're identical twins.

Nathaniel (*irritably*) No we're not!

Obadiah Oh yes we are . . .

Dame All right, all right! We've done that bit! You are both Stupid anyway.

Nathaniel That's right.

Obadiah Very true.

Dame Well, I can't keep calling you both Stupid, can I? And you've got such long names. Here, haven't you got any nicknames?

Nathaniel Oh, you can call me Nat. That's short for Nathaniel.

Obadiah I'm known as Nob.

Dame Really? . . . Why's that then?

Obadiah Because I've got a——

Nathaniel (*interrupting hastily*) It's short for Obadiah.

Dame Hmmm. Nat and Nob eh? And you both work for the Witchfinder General, do you?

Obadiah Oh, he's 'orrible. 'ORRIBLE!

Dame How does he find his witches then?

Nathaniel He smells 'em out!

Obadiah And then his assistant, Smallpiece, pokes them with his sniffer.

Dame (*incredulous*) What, you mean he wipes his nose on them?!

Nathaniel No, no. He gives them a poke with a pin where they can't feel it, and if they don't yelp, he accuses them and that's that! Off to the dungeons. Once they're in there they confess soon enough, and then it's "frying tonight"!

Dame What do you mean?

Obadiah (*ghoulishly*) Burned at the stake!

Dame Ooooh! How 'orrible. Self-basting 'umans!

Nathaniel Look out! Here he comes now!

Grimnasty and Smallpiece enter through the audience, sniffing

Witchfinder Ah! I like to get amongst the common people. And this lot are a lot more common than usual!

Audience participation

Smell that, Smallpiece? The rank odour of squalor. Nothing quite like it. And look at some of these faces. It's like walking through a cabbage patch!

Audience participation

Greetings humble peasants! Who has any information to impart? What about you, simpleton? Have you any witches to report? No? Well, I don't imagine there's much room for information if you've got a brain the size of a pea! Anyone with any Christmas decorations? No madam, I am not selling Cornettos . . . *etc. etc.* (*He catches sight of the three outside Dame Dumplings' Cottage*) Aha! You've caught a suspect! Well done!

Dame Eh?

Witchfinder We shall interrogate her at once! (*He calls*) Old woman!

Dame (*looking around*) Where?

Witchfinder (*approaching her*) You! Old woman!

Dame Watch it pal . . .

Witchfinder Mmmmm . . . I smell . . . I smell . . .

Dame (*to the audience*) He does. He smells.

Witchfinder (*melodramatically*) I smell—WITCHERY!

Dame Are you sure it's not my aftershave lotion?

Witchfinder Tell me, old woman, is that your little house?

Dame Yep.

Witchfinder So that must be your broom then?

Dame (*carefully*) Yes.

Witchfinder And I daresay you live on your own, do you?

Dame Oh no . . .

Witchfinder (*disappointedly*) Oh.

Dame Me, live on my own? Ha! What an idea. I should say not. Course I
  don't live on my own . . .

Pause

  I live with my cat.

Witchfinder Your cat?!!

Dame Beelzebub.

Witchfinder Beelzebub?!!

Dame (*fondly*) He's a little devil you know . . .

Witchfinder A DEVIL!!!

Dame (*smacking her ear*) I seem to have developed an echo.

Witchfinder Aaaargh! A witch! A witch!

Dame Which? What? Where?

Witchfinder (*pointing an accusatory finger*) WITCH!

Dame Which what? Which car? Which computer? Which way to the public
  bar? What are you on about?

Witchfinder (*sinisterly*) I think this may call for a little sniffer . . .

Dame (*aside*) A little stinker . . .

Witchfinder Smallpiece!

Dame Yes, that's him.

Witchfinder Prepare the sniffer . . .

Dame Ooooh! Really! Don't look children! I thought this was a family
  show!

Witchfinder Old woman. Smallpiece is going to sniff you.

Dame (*grabbing him by the lapels and lifting him on to tiptoes*) Listen Fatso,
  if he comes near me with his little sniffer, he'll never smell again! Geddit?!

*At which point Emma, Sir Daniel and the village children enter. Emma
carries a covered basket. Their laughter dies as they see the Witchfinder and
his men*

Emma Auntie, Auntie! Oh . . . I . . . er . . .

Witchfinder (*immediately losing interest in the Dame*) Well, well, well . . . And who have we here?

Dame My niece Emma, and a . . . er . . . (*She gestures with her head for Sir Daniel to clear off*)

But he simply stares at her in puzzlement
  (*Finally giving up*) And a humble woodcutter.

Witchfinder I see. (*He slips into melodrama*) And why are you in such a hurry, my pretty?

Emma Er . . . I . . .

Witchfinder Ah! I spy a basket . . .

Dame (*aside*) That makes two of us . . .

Witchfinder Wait! (*He sniffs ostentatiously*) I can smell something! (*His nose is drawn to the basket*) What have you got in there?

Emma Er . . . fruit! I've been gathering fresh fruit in the forest!

Witchfinder In December?

Emma (*thinking fast*) I went to Waitrose! (*Or other local supermarket*)

Witchfinder (*poking his hand into the basket*) Aaargh! (*He pulls out a paper chain*) Decorations!

Emma Oh dear.

Witchfinder (*gleefully, pulling out a cracker*) Crackers!

Dame (*aside*) You certainly are, mate . . .

Witchfinder Mince pies!!!

All ONLY TEN PENCE EACH IN THE INTERVAL, FROM THE REAR OF THE AUDITORIUM! (*Or other refreshments point*)

Witchfinder (*triumphantly*) You're planning a Christmas party! Caught red-handed! Ha ha ha ha!!

Dame We've been rumbled.

Emma Oh dear, oh dear.

Witchfinder Seize her!

Sir Daniel steps forward into the path of Nathaniel and Obadiah. He pulls Emma back behind him

Sir Daniel (*manfully*) Hold!

Witchfinder What?!

Sir Daniel (*to Grimnasty*) Don't lay a filthy hand on her, you snivelling, traitorous, crop-headed scoundrel!

Witchfinder (*politely*) Do I know you?

Sir Daniel Er . . . no.

Witchfinder You're not by any chance a bold and gallant cavalier, who has just helped Prince Charles escape to France, now cunningly disguised as a humble woodcutter, are you?!

Sir Daniel Er . . . well . . . actually . . .

Emma (*stepping in front of Sir Daniel*) No! He is not! (*Melodramatically*) Come, Sir Witchfinder! I am the guilty one, I confess, I'll come quietly. (*She holds up her hands as if for handcuffs*)

Witchfinder Ha ha ha ha!! Bring her then!

Audience participation as Nathaniel and Obadiah move to take her arms

Smallpiece (*who has moved over to Dame Dumplings, and is regarding her with unnatural interest*) Er ... what about the witch, Your Malignance?
Witchfinder What witch?
Smallpiece (*tugging on the Dame's sleeve*) This one!
Witchfinder Oh yes, her. Well, we'll come back for her later. But now, I have important business to attend to. To the dungeons!! Ha ha ha!!
Emma (*piteously*) Auntie!

Audience participation as Grimnasty, Smallpiece, Nathaniel and Obadiah exit with the struggling Emma

Dame (*sobbing*) Oh Emma! What a heroine! Boo hoo! My poor little Emma, in the hands of the evil Witchfinder and his creepy little friend with the sniffer! Boo hoo hoo! Boo hoo hoo!
Sir Daniel (*comforting her*) Don't worry Dame Dumplings. We'll rescue Emma. Everything will be all right. You have my word as a cavalier!
Dame Boo hoo hoo. Fat lot of use that is. You probably said that to the King before they cut his 'ead orf! Boo hoo hoo! This is all your fault anyway! Oh boo hoo hoo!
Sir Daniel (*pacing*) I think I have a plan ...
Dame Oh no! Boo hoo hoo! (*She pauses*) What?
Sir Daniel I'll tell you later. We'll get Emma back from Grimnasty's evil clutches, AND we'll throw the best Christmas party you've ever seen!
Dame (*snivelling*) Really?
Sir Daniel Really! God save the King!
All look at him in puzzlement
Well, the Prince then ...
All Hurray!

Song (Dame, Sir Daniel and Village Children)
CURTAIN

ACT II

The castle dungeon

Sinister music and distant gibbering screams mingle with an incessant dripping noise in the dark. The gloomy vault is hung with grisly remains and fiendish contraptions. A single shaft of light from high overhead illuminates Emma. She is sitting c in the stocks, which are raised up on a block. She is loaded with chains, and has a large, brightly coloured handkerchief tied around her face. She struggles furiously as Smallpiece gleefully tickles her feet with a large feather

Smallpiece (*to the audience*) This is fun! Shall I carry on?

Audience participation, during which:

Grimnasty enters

Witchfinder Ha ha ha ha! Well now, my pretty!
Smallpiece (*simpering*) Thank you, M'Lud, but I'm not looking my best.
Witchfinder Not you, imbecile! (*He regards Emma*) Well, have you learned anything from her yet?
Smallpiece She won't talk, M'Lud.
Witchfinder Nothing?
Smallpiece (*emphatically*) Not a squeak!
Emma Mmmmff!
Witchfinder Smallpiece, have you tried removing the handkerchief?
Smallpiece Er . . .
Witchfinder (*shouting*) Take it off, you numbskull!!

Smallpiece hurriedly removes the gag

Now then. What have you to say for yourself, my pretty?
Emma Nothing!
Witchfinder Ha ha ha ha! Such defiance! But you'll talk!

Audience participation

Emma (*bravely*) Never!
Witchfinder Ha! You'll soon change your tune. Tell me where and when the Village Christmas Party will take place, or it'll be the worse for you!
Emma I'll never tell you, never! You don't scare me, and you don't scare them either, does he, boys and girls?!

Audience participation

Witchfinder Very well! Don't say I didn't warn you! Smallpiece! I think we'll start with the thumbscrews!

Smallpiece (*happily*) The thumbscrews M'Lud!

Comic business as they find the thumbscrews are stuck on Smallpiece, and then become stuck on Grimnasty as well. They eventually separate after a violent struggle, during which Grimnasty places his boot in a sensitive area of his assistant's anatomy

Witchfinder Let's try the red hot coals, shall we?

Smallpiece Er... Couldn't get red hot coals, M'Lud. (*Peering at a bag*) Will economy charcoal briquettes do?

Witchfinder (*patiently*) Never mind. It'll have to be the burning poker instead then!

Smallpiece Burning poker, certainly M'Lud.

Witchfinder This is going to hurt me, a lot more than it's going to hurt you ...

Smallpiece, still wearing the thumbscrews, clumsily hands him the glowing end of the poker. Grimnasty drops it with a yell, and clutches his hand

Smallpiece (*interestedly*) So it did!

Witchfinder Get out you imbecile! And fetch the Great Book of Inquisition and Endless Torment!

Smallpiece Not the nineteen eighty-nine *Blue Peter Annual?* (*Or other topical publication*)

Witchfinder The Reader's Digest Torture Manual, you idiot! (*He continues clutching his hand*)

Smallpiece exits

Now then, let's try again, shall we? I'd like you to tell me about the Village Christmas Party. If you won't, I'm going to make you confess to being a witch.

Emma Never! I won't, it isn't true!

Witchfinder We'll see. After you've spent a few nights down here in the dark, with rats and spiders for company, you'll change your mind! Ha ha ha ha!!!

Audience participation as:

Smallpiece returns with a large, dusty, leatherbound volume under his arm Aha! The Great Book of Inquisition and Endless Torment! Now then my pretty, I'd like you to take a look at this! ...

Smallpiece melodramatically opens the book to reveal a large and horrible picture of Cilla Black—or other infamous celebrity

Emma Oh no! No! Please! Not that!

Witchfinder Ha ha ha ha! And this! ...

Large and horrible picture of Tom O'Connor

Emma I can't stand it! Mercy! Please!
Witchfinder Then confess!
Emma No, no, you heartless fiend!
Witchfinder Then take that! ...

Large and horrible picture of Bonnie Langford

Emma Aaaaargh! All right! All right! I give in! (*Sobbing*) What do you want of me?
Witchfinder (*triumphantly*) Ha ha ha! That's better! (*He moves to stand behind her*) Well, to start with, I want you to watch this little bauble ...

He starts to hypnotize her. After a few moments both Emma and Smallpiece have become mesmerized, moving their heads in time with the swinging pendant

The Lights fade to Black-out

<h2 style="text-align:center">SCENE 2</h2>

The village

Peter Farthing enters, looking around him

Peter (*calling*) Bottom? Bottom?! (*Then, to the audience*) Oh, hallo there, I'm still searching for my Bottom. You haven't seen him have you?

Audience participation

Dear oh dear. Where can he have got to? It's just not like him to disappear like this ...

The village children enter

Girl Peter, Peter! Dame Dumplings is coming, and she's really, really upset!
Boy She keeps crying. It's like the wailing wall!
Girl More like the blubbering mountain!
Boy More like a mountain of blubber!

The children all laugh

Peter (*sternly*) Now then! If Dame Dumplings is upset, what must we be?
Boy Pleased?
Peter Sympathetic! We must be polite and kind, mustn't we?
Children (*chorus*) Yes Peter ...
Peter And we mustn't be horrible, or poke fun, must we?
Children (*chorus*) No Peter ...
Peter Right then.

Dame Dumplings enters, sniffing horribly

Dame Hallo kids ...
Children (*chorus*) Hallo Fatso!

Boy Did you know that when you've been crying, you look even more repulsive than usual?

Dame Boo hoo hoo! Boo hoo hoo. Everyone is so horrible to me. And me, with my poor, dear, little Emma in the hands of the evil Witchfinder too! Oh boo hoo hoo! And where's that bold and gallant cavalier got to? He was supposed to have effected a spectacular rescue by now! (*She snivels*)

Peter (*glaring at the children*) There, there, Dame Dumplings. Don't be sad. Nothing's ever that bad. Here, dry your eyes with this.

He hands her a pristine handkerchief, on which she proceeds to blow her nose in a particularly disgusting fashion

Here, why don't you help me to look for my Bottom?

Dame (*snivelling*) It's behind you ...

Peter (*declining the return of the handkerchief*) No, no. Not that bottom. I'm talking about my dancing bear.

Dame Oh don't start that again!

Peter My BEAR that DANCES!

Dame (*realization dawning*) Oh! Oh, you don't mean a great, big, black, hairy brute, with big, huge paws, little, beady eyes, and a sort of long, brownish snout do you?!

Peter (*excitedly*) Yes! Yes, that's him!

Dame (*morosely*) Haven't seen him.

Peter (*disappointed*) Oh.

Dame I wish I could help, but ... but I ... Boo hoo hoo!

Peter Dear me, you really do seem to be a bit down.

Dame Down?! I'm nearly down and out, mate! You don't seem to appreciate that my poor Emma has been grabbed by the Roundheads!

Peter (*wincing*) Nasty!

Dame Very nasty! She's probably being strung up by her toes at this very moment!

Peter Oh, I'm sure they won't mistreat her. I'll wager she'll be back by Christmas. You'll find a way to get her out. Things are never that bad. Remember ...

Song (Peter, Dame and Children)

Dame That's all very well, but HOW am I going to get her out?

Peter If you ask me, you need to consult the Wise Women of (*insert local town or place*).

Dame You don't mean the Witches of (*same place*)?!!!

Dramatic chord

Peter Yes!

Dame Oh no. I couldn't go to them. It'd ruin my credibility as a wise woman.

Peter Ah well. Don't say I didn't tell you. I must go and look for Bottom now. Oh, and if you should see him, I'd keep well clear if I were you. He can turn a bit funny when I'm not about ...

Peter exits with the children

Dame (*to the audience*) Ha! Bottom! That's the least of my worries. Great big, fat, soppy bundle of fur! Couldn't fight his way out of a wet paper bag that bear. He makes Winnie the Pooh look positively ferocious. Makes Paddington look like Norman Tebbit. (*Or other much feared personality*)

Meanwhile, a bear (Sir Daniel in disguise) enters and lumbers up behind her

Audience participation

What's that? I know me bottom's behind me. There's enough of it!

Comic business with the bear and the Dame, until they suddenly end up face to face

Aaaaargh! A bear! I didn't mean it, really! Nice teddy ... please don't eat me, you wouldn't like me ... much too fatty. (*Desperately*) Er ... I understand you dance? ...

Sir Daniel (*in muffled tones*) Dame Dumplings, it's me!

Dame Aaaargh! A talking bear! I'm going bonkers!

The bear removes its head to reveal Sir Daniel

Sir Daniel No, no. It's me. This is part of my plan. Another cunning disguise!

Dame (*collapsing with relief*) Well it's a sight more cunning than the last one! (*Hastily*) Not that it had me fooled for a moment of course ...

Sir Daniel Why are you shaking?

Dame I'm not! Anyway, what's this plan of yours then?

Sir Daniel Aha! We shall infiltrate the castle, in the guise of a performing bear and its keeper, come to entertain the garrison. Once within the lofty bastion, I shall effect an escape, locate the dungeons, and rescue Emma, whilst you create a diversion in the opposite direction. Emma and I will then escape.

Dame You will?

Sir Daniel Of course.

Dame And where does that leave me may I ask? I'll tell you. Stuck in Castle Dracula with a lot of real evil geezers and their little sniffers that's where! I mean, don't you think they'll be just a little suspicious?

Sir Daniel (*airily*) Oh no. Shouldn't think so.

Dame (*sceptically*) No?

Sir Daniel (*emphatically*) No.

Dame Hmmm. Doesn't sound too watertight to me, but I suppose it's worth a try.

Sir Daniel Stout woman! I'll meet you at eight, by the castle gate!

He exits

Dame I won't be late, mate! Oi! Hang on a minute! What do you mean "stout woman"?!

She exits

SCENE 3

The village—later

Grimnasty, Smallpiece and Nathaniel enter through the audience, to audience participation

Witchfinder Well, well, well. A motley gathering of the local peasantry! What a rude and ugly crew! I shall question them closely.

He addresses the audience, who are participating loudly!

Greetings, simple rustics! I am seeking the venue of the Village Christmas Party. Perhaps one of you will be good enough to tell me where it will take place?

Audience participation

Bah! You miserable underlings! I don't need your feeble help anyway. My new assistant will tell me all I need to know! Bring her!

Emma enters, zombie-like, through the audience. She is obviously hypnotized. Obadiah trails along behind her, clearly fascinated by her condition. She reaches Grimnasty and turns to face the audience. Her face is blank

Ha ha ha ha!!! Now then Emma. Listen very carefully . . .

Nathaniel ⎱
Obadiah ⎰ (*together*) I shall say zis, only once . . .

Witchfinder You know where the Christmas Party is to be held, don't you?
Emma (*compliantly*) Yes, Nicholas.
Witchfinder Are you going to tell me where it is?

Audience participation

Emma Yes Nicholas.
Witchfinder (*gloating*) Ha ha ha ha!!!
Emma (*evilly*) Ha ha ha ha!!!

All look at her in extreme surprise

Witchfinder Er . . . yes . . . where is it then?
Emma (*flinging out her arm and knocking Grimnasty's hat off*) There! At the house of my aunt!
Witchfinder Ha! Splendid! Then we'll catch the whole rascally gang in one fell swoop, and they can all spend the rest of Christmas languishing in my dungeons! Ha ha ha ha!!

Emma joins in the evil laughter enthusiastically. Smallpiece looks extremely put out

I can hardly wait! Come! Back to the castle. I must lay my trap! Ha ha ha ha!!!

They exit to audience participation, Emma flourishing her cloak wickedly, in the same fashion as Grimnasty

SCENE 4

Near the castle walls

It is dark and windy. Dame Dumplings can be seen pacing in the gloom, thinly disguised as a performing bear's keeper

Dame (*muttering*) "I'll meet you at eight, by the castle gate!" Ha! So much for that! It must be at least half-past, and not a sign of the bold and gallant performing bear! Oh bother me broomstick! Where's he got to?!

Bottom enters

There you are! Where have you been?! I've been waiting here for absolutely ages! Gives me the creeps this place. I feel like a stray cat hanging around a Chinese take-away!

Bottom looks interested at the mention of food

Well?! What are you peering at, Bungle?! Let's get on with it, before I change my mind.

Bottom Growwwl ...

Dame Nasty touch of wind you've got there, Furbag. I'd lay off the radishes if I were you!

Bottom Grrowwwwl ...

Dame Oho! Playing the part are we? Right, come on then Baloo, let's see you do a dance!

Bottom obligingly performs a small dance

Well, that's not going to fool anyone, is it?! Is that the best you can do? You look more like a dancing hippopotamus than a dancing bear!

Bottom (*menacingly*) Grrrrowwwwl!!!

Dame And you can lay off the ferocious carnivore bit with me, mate! It won't wash! I mean just look at you!

Bottom examines himself in puzzlement

No self-respecting bear would be seen dead in an 'orrible, scraggy, motheaten coat like that!

Bottom (*enraged*) GRRRROWWWWL!!!

Dame Come along, no nonsense! Go and give your fur a good brush down! I'll wait here for you. And don't come back until you're respectable!

She pushes a perplexed-looking Bottom off

Bottom exits one side, as:

Sir Daniel enters on the other, his bear's head under his arm

I don't know! These aristocrats! It's no wonder they lost the war. (*She sees Sir Daniel*) Ooer! That was quick! Must have gone to Sketchley's! (*Or other local cleaners*)

Sir Daniel (*impatiently*) There you are! I've been waiting for you by the other gate for half an hour!

Dame Oh! That's why you were late is it? Here, have you brushed your fur now? (*Inspecting him*) Oh yes, that's much better. Quite respectable really. Almost like a real bear!

Sir Daniel Eh? (*He looks puzzled but places on his bear's head*) Right, come along then, as quietly as possible! (*He starts to lead off*)

Dame (*adjusting her feeble disguise*) All right, all right! Keep your fur on! (*To the audience*) Flaming nobility. Leave you hanging around for hours, then expect you to jump to it, as soon as they click their fingers! That's just typical isn't it? I don't know really ... Tut tut ...

At which point the real Bottom lumbers back on behind them

Sir Daniel (*crossly*) Shhh!

Dame (*loudly*) Pardon?

Sir Daniel Shhhhh!

Dame (*back to him*) Shhhhh!

Sir Daniel SHHHHH!!

Dame (*to Bottom*) SHHHHH!!

Bottom SHHGRRRRRH!!

Sir Daniel
Dame (*turning; together*) SSSSSHHHHHHHHHHHH!!! (*They see Bottom*) Aaaaaaaargh!!!

Dame It's a bear! A ruddy great bear!

Dame and Sir Daniel run off

Bottom looks rather mournful, attracting the sympathy of an impressionable audience. He performs a sad little dance, then exits

SCENE 5

The village

Nathaniel and Obadiah enter

Obadiah (*singing*) "Away in a manger ..."

Nathaniel (*irritably*) Look, will you shut up?!

Obadiah I can't help it Nat. It keeps going round inside my head ...

Nathaniel (*rudely*) Well it's got plenty of room for manœuvre, hasn't it!

Obadiah (*unabashed*) Nat ... I've been thinking ...

Nathaniel And?

Obadiah Hurts, doesn't it.

Nathaniel Look! Will you please try and concentrate?! We have got to find Dame Dumplings and warn her that her party has been rumbled!

Obadiah Have we? Why?

Nathaniel Well you liked her, didn't you? She seemed like quite a decent old bird, didn't she? Anyway, I don't like to think of that young slip of a girl under old Grimnasty's evil influence. She keeps cackling like an extra from *Dawn of the Zombie Flesh-Eaters*! It just doesn't seem right!

Dame Dumplings enters, caterwauling

Dame Boo hoo hoo! I'm so unhappy!

Nathaniel Unhappy? Why?

Dame Why?! Why? he says! Why d'you think, you great berk?! My darling little niece Emma has been slung in chokey by the Hooded Claw! I've been labelled a witch! And I've just had a close encounter with a man-eating bear than Grizzly Adams!!! Oh it's all too much! Boo hoo hoo!

Nathaniel Oh no! Please Dame Dumplings, don't cry . . .

Dame (*sniffing horribly*) Why not? . . .

Nathaniel Well it makes you look all ugly. Your face gets all screwed up and wrinkled, and your eyes go all red and piggy . . .

Obadiah (*helpfully*) Same as usual really . . .

Dame (*stricken*) Ohhhh! Boo hoo hoo!!!

Nathaniel Shut up Obadiah! Really! That's no way to speak to a woman of her age!

Dame (*outraged*) What do you mean "her age"?! You think I'm old, don't you? Go on, admit it!

Nathaniel Er . . . no, no! I don't. Really. Just a bit, well . . . lived in . . . that's all . . .

Obadiah Like a delapidated hovel.

Dame Eh?!

Nathaniel (*hastily*) Dame Dumplings, listen! I have to tell you about your niece!

Dame (*hitching up her voluminous skirts*) My knees? What's wrong with my knees?!

Nathaniel No no no! Your niece. Emma.

Dame Oh my poor little Emma! Ensnared by the evil Witchfinder! But she'll never crack, not my Emma! She's made of the right stuff! The same stuff as me!

Obadiah Lard?

Dame (*ignoring the interruption*) She'll never grass! She's no squealer! She won't——

Nathaniel (*interrupting*) Dame Dumplings!

Dame What?

Nathaniel She talked.

Dame No! I won't believe it! Not my Emma! Oh they must have mistreated her something cruel! No, don't tell me the grisly details! Oh they must have stretched her on the rack . . .

Nathaniel Worse than that . . .

Dame Oh no! Not hung upside down in a pit of venomous snakes?

Obadiah Worse than that . . .

Dame No! They didn't force her to eat a portion of Kentucky Fried Chicken, did they?!

Nathaniel Worse than that . . .

Dame (*amazed*) What could be worse than that?

Nathaniel (*darkly*) Hypnotism!

Dame Eh?

Nathaniel She's under the evil influence!

Dame Oh no! I warned her! I told her drinking all that scrumpy would land her in trouble! I——

Nathaniel Not alcohol! Hypnotism! Grimnasty has her in his power. He has hypnotized her!

Dame Hypnot ... hypno ... hyp ... Oh the villain!

Nathaniel And she's spilled the beans. He knows exactly when and where the Village Christmas Party's going to be held, and he's going to be the most unwelcome gatecrasher you've ever met!

Dame Oh gawd! What am I going to do?!

Nathaniel Cancel the party for starters!

Dame Cancel the party! Never! I can't do that! All the invitations have been sent! I'd never contact all the guests in time. They'll all turn up wearing their little party hats, only to find Dastardly and Mutley waiting for them with the paddy wagon!

Nathaniel (*conspiratorially*) Then you'll have to get rid of him.

Dame What?

Obadiah You know ... Get rid of him ...

Dame What with? Vanishing lotion?

Obadiah (*whispering*) Put a spell on him.

Dame (*whispering*) How?

Obadiah Well I don't know, you're the witch!

Dame (*grabbing Obadiah and shaking him*) NO I'M NOT!!!!

Nathaniel All right, all right! You'll have to consult the Wise Women of (*local town or place*) then.

Dame You don't mean, the Witches of (*same place*)?!!

Dramatic chord

Nathaniel Er ... yes.

Dame 'Ere! If you know about the Witches of (*same place*), how come you haven't nicked 'em?

Nathaniel Leave off! That'd be dangerous that would!

Obadiah We don't have no truck with REAL witches!

Nathaniel No fear! WE don't want to end up as slimy toads!

They exit hastily

Dame (*calling after them*) Oh ... right ... thanks for your help.

Sir Daniel enters, still wearing his bear's head

Sir Daniel I say! What did those rascally Roundheaded rogues want?!

Dame I'll tell you later! Come on, it's time you and I consulted the Witches of (*local town or place*) ...

Sir Daniel Not that place with all the estate agents! (*Or other local joke*)

Dame That's it. Come on.

They exit

SCENE 6

The village

Peter Farthing enters

Peter (*calling*) Bottom! Bottom! Oh where is he? (*To the audience*) You haven't seen him have you?

Audience participation

Have you? Well, I can't see him now, but I'm sure he's somewhere around here. Tell you what, how would you like to help me catch him?

Audience participation

Right then, here's what we'll do: I'll go and hide in Dame Dumplings' cottage until he comes along. When you see him, I want you all to shout out to him. Will you do that?

Audience participation

Good! You can shout out loud, because he's very friendly, not at all fierce really. So when you see him, you all shout out "Kiss me Bottom!" All right? Let's try now. One, two, three . . .

Audience participation

Well that was quite good, but you'll have to be a lot louder than that, because he's got furry ears and doesn't hear too well. So, let's try again shall we? After three. One, two, three . . .

Audience participation

Very good! That's much better! But someone shouted "Kiss me bum!" didn't they? . . . Oh it was you was it, sonny? Now you mustn't call him that, because he won't take kindly to it at all! Right. I'm going to hide now. Don't forget, when you see Bottom, shout out loud!

Peter exits into Dame Dumplings' cottage

After a few moments, Bottom wanders on, noisily eating a mince pie

All KISS ME BOTTOM!

Bottom drops his mince pie, rushes up to the front row of the audience, and starts kissing selected victims

Peter dashes on

Peter Where is he? Did you see him?

Audience participation as Bottom endeavours to hide in their midst, by sitting on top of one of them

I know! We'll sing his favourite song, shall we? He'll come then. He can't resist it!

Song (Peter)

By the end of which, Bottom is dancing merrily around, and is easily caught by his master

Come on then, old fellow. Now I've finally found you, we've got some rehearsal to catch up on. There's a performance at the castle tonight. Entertainment for the garrison. They're a miserable bunch, still, the show must go on! Well cheerio kids, and thanks for all your help!

There is a rumble of distant thunder. The Lights dim

Sounds like a nasty storm brewing! We'd best get under cover ... I wouldn't like to be caught out tonight ...

They exit

It grows darker still. Thunder crashes and lightning flashes. The wind howls. The sound of driving rain is heard

Dame Dumplings and Sir Daniel enter through the audience, cloaks pulled closely around them against the weather

Sir Daniel (*shouting over the wind and rain*) So who are these Wise Women then?!

Dame (*stopping*) Look! Let's get this straight shall we? They're not "Wise Women", they're flaming witches! Three ugly hags!

Sir Daniel Bananarama? (*Or other tropical trio*)

Dame I said OLD hags ...

Sir Daniel Ah! The weird sisters!

Dame I dunno if they're related, but they're certainly weird!

Sir Daniel You don't seem to be overly fond of them?

Dame Neither will you be mate, when you've met 'em! They're the sort that gets us Wise Women a bad name—always interfering with toads and mucking about with stinkwort. And they're so ugly! You've never seen anything like it!

Sir Daniel Worse than you?

Dame Infinitely!

Sir Daniel How appalling ...

Dame (*preoccupied*) And I'm, always worried that they'll be so jealous of my great beauty, that they'll cast an 'orrible spell on me ...

Sir Daniel I should set your mind at rest on that score, Dame Dumplings.

Dame Yes, well, maybe ... Aha! They're up ahead!

Sir Daniel How do you know?

Dame I can smell their foul brew!

Sir Daniel Can't make a decent cuppa, eh?

Dame No no no! Their brew in their cauldron.

Sir Daniel Ah! Witches' cauldron. Vile potions, eh?

Dame (*morosely*) Probably.

They exit

SCENE 7

A mountain top wreathed in mist

Thunder rolls ominously, and strange lights can be seen. As a wolf howls nearby, we see three aged crones, huddled around an enormous cauldron which is belching foul green smoke. They are none other than the three crones Sir Daniel encountered in the forest

All   Hubble bubble, toil and trouble,
               Trouble, hubble, boil and muddle!
1st Witch Oh cut it out will you! How's that cream of asparagus soup coming on?
2nd Witch (*tasting the pot*) Needs a bit more salt.
3rd Witch (*adding salt*) Here we are then . . .
1st Witch Aiiii! Wait! I see . . . I see a tall, mysterious stranger approaching, in the company of a fat, loathsome reptile!
2nd Witch (*admiringly*) Ah! You have the vision, sister!
1st Witch (*caustically*) Don't be such a silly cow! I can see them coming up the path over there! Look!
3rd Witch Oh yes! It's that bloke who was dressed up as a woodcutter.
2nd Witch What's he dressed as now then?
3rd Witch A pansy I think. And he's got old Mistress Wobblebottom in tow!
1st Witch Righto, here we go girls, into the routine!
All (*wailing horribly*) Ohhhhhhhhhh!

Sir Daniel and Dame Dumplings enter

1st Witch Hail!
2nd Witch Hail!!
3rd Witch Hail!!!
Dame (*drily*) I should have brought my umbrella.
Witches   Fair is foul and foul is fair,
               Welcome to this witches' lair!
               (*They cackle manically*)
               Harrgh, harrgh, harrgh!!!
Dame (*to Sir Daniel*) Bit over the top I think . . .
Sir Daniel Definitely.
Dame Listen girls, there's only room for one ham in this show, and I'm it, geddit?!
1st Witch (*in her normal voice*) Fair enough.
Dame Right. Where were we?
1st Witch Misery!
2nd Witch Misery!!
3rd Witch Misery!!!
Dame (*aside*) And "woe" I shouldn't wonder?
1st Witch And woe!!!
Dame Thought as much!

1st Witch Ohhhh!

2nd Witch Ohhhhhh!!

3rd Witch Ohhhhhhhh!!!

Dame If you don't stop wailing, you'll be reported to Greenpeace! (*To the audience*) Whaling! Greenpeace! Geddit?! Oh, never mind!

Sir Daniel Fair maidens of (*local place*) we are seeking——

1st Witch (*interrupting rudely*) We KNOW why you and this "lady" have come here!

Dame You do?

1st Witch Yes! And we don't sell love potions!!!

Witches (*cackling*) Har, har, har!

Dame (*stiffly*) We haven't come for a love potion.

1st Witch No?

Dame No. We want you to cast a spell on someone.

1st Witch Who?

Dame The Witchfinder General!

Witches (*aghast*) THE WITCHFINDER GENERAL?!!!!

1st Witch Not THE Witchfinder General?!!

Dame Yes. THE Witchfinder General! And he's in the vicinity right now! So if you don't want to find yourselves being grilled—in more ways than one—you'd better come up with a spell pretty fast!

1st Witch What sort of spell?

Dame Well I don't know, wartfeatures! You're the witch! Turn him into something!

2nd Witch I have it! Sometimes large and slimy . . .

Dame Yes, that's it . . .

3rd Witch Shapeless and squishy . . .

Dame You're getting the idea . . .

2nd Witch An evil-looking sludge!

1st Witch You don't mean . . .

3rd Witch Yes! A McDonald's milkshake!

Dame Hang on a minute . . .

2nd Witch Or a cheeseburger!

1st Witch (*getting carried away*) Or an Egg McMuffin!

Dame No no no! I don't want him turned into fast food! Don't you do amphibians? I mean, what about a nice newt or tadpole or something?

3rd Witch Tricky . . .

2nd Witch Very tricky . . .

1st Witch We can do a horny toad.

Dame Really! I think a common toad would be more appropriate. We don't want him having any fun!

1st Witch But the ingredients are difficult to come by. And expensive . . .

2nd Witch Very expensive . . .

3rd Witch Very, very expensive . . .

Dame All right, how much?

Witches LOADSA MONEY!!!

Sir Daniel (*intervening*) Good women of (*local place*), the only money I have is this silver penny . . .

1st Witch (*snatching it*) That'll do nicely!

Sir Daniel It bears the head of our late King Charles ...

2nd Witch (*examining it*) Really? Wouldn't have thought it would fit on there would you?

3rd Witch No. You'd have thought they'd have put it on a plate wouldn't you?

1st Witch I thought they put it on a spike!

All cackle hysterically

Sir Daniel Where is the spell?

1st Witch (*handing over a scrap of paper*) Here we are dearie, it's all written on there ...

Sir Daniel What do I have to do?

2nd Witch Just read it aloud, and hurl the ingredients at the recipient.

Sir Daniel What if he won't stand still?

3rd Witch He will! Once you have named him in the spell, he will be held motionless until the end of the incantation!

Sir Daniel Hmmm. And what are the ingredients?

2nd Witch A lock of hair from a virgin ...

Sir Daniel What?!!

1st Witch I told you they were difficult to come by ...

Dame Well don't look at me!

3rd Witch A gallon of frogspawn ...

Dame I think I might have a jar of frogspawn in my larder ...

Sir Daniel Eeeyuch!

1st Witch And a kiss, stolen from a pretty girl ...

Dame (*pursing her lips*) Ready when you are, Danny Boy!

Sir Daniel (*tactfully*) Er ... that wouldn't be stealing though, would it?

Dame (*disgruntled*) S'pose not ...

1st Witch It wouldn't be pretty either!

They all cackle again

Dame Right! Thank you "ladies". I think we've got all we need. Come along Sir Daniel, before you get corrupted!

Dame and Sir Daniel exit

Witches   Fair is foul and foul is fair,
　　　　　　Eye of stoat and nose of hare ...

Song (The Three Witches)

After which, the Three Witches exit

SCENE 8

The castle: the Witchfinder General's chambers

Grimnasty is slouched indolently on his throne C, *flanked by Smallpiece and Emma*

Witchfinder Ha ha ha ha!! I can't wait to see the faces of those idiotic villagers when I turn up at their Christmas Party! ha ha ha ha!!!

Audience participation

Emma (*evilly*) Ha ha ha ha!!

Smallpiece (*sullenly*) I wish you'd stop her laughing like that! It isn't natural.

Witchfinder Bah! Don't be such a baby, Smallpiece! You're only jealous!

Emma Of course he is, My Lord! A jealous baby! Make me your first assistant. Let me wield the little sniffer! Ha ha ha ha!!

Witchfinder Er . . . Yes, well, we'll have to see. Anyway, as I was saying . . .

There is a knock. Nathaniel and Obadiah enter

Nathaniel Dame Dumplings and A. Woodcutter to see you, M'Lud. They seek an audience.

Witchfinder (*gesturing to the audience*) They can have this one! They're no good anyway!

Audience participation

Nathaniel No no, Your Evilness. They've come about the girl. To plead for clemency.

Witchfinder Clemency? She's not called Clemency!

Nathaniel To plead for mercy, Your Unpleasantness.

Witchfinder Really.

Obadiah No, not really. Actually they've come to transform you into a——

Nathaniel (*hissing*) Shut up!

Witchfinder Mercy indeed! Ha! I don't know the meaning of the word!

Obadiah (*helpfully*) Well, it sort of means being kind and forgiving and——

Witchfinder (*shouting*) Silence, cretin! When will these peasants learn that I have no mercy! Ha ha ha!

Emma Ha ha ha ha!!!

Smallpiece (*surlily*) Oh har har har.

Witchfinder (*glaring at Smallpiece*) Show them in!

Nathaniel and Obadiah usher on Sir Daniel and Dame Dumplings, then hastily exit

(*To Dame*) So, foul harridan! We meet again!

Sir Daniel (*espying Emma*) Emma! Emma! (*He rushes to embrace her*) Are you unharmed?!

Emma Unhand me, sir!

Sir Daniel (*perplexed*) But Emma?

Emma My Lord! This man is no humble woodcutter! He is a rascally and malignant cavalier, who has recently helped the Prince escape to France!

Sir Daniel (*stunned by this betrayal*) Emma!

Witchfinder Indeed? Well, we know how to deal with Royalist vermin don't we? Ha ha ha ha!!!

Emma joins in the laughter. Smallpiece looks obstinate

Smallpiece!

Smallpiece jumps with fright, and laughs obligingly

Go and prepare our dampest dungeon for our new guest—although he won't be staying long! I have a feeling he's going to lose his head! Ha ha ha ha!!!!

Audience participation, as Emma joins in the laughter again, whilst . . .

Smallpiece exits scowling

Dame Now listen here, Dirty Den! (*Or other topical villain*) Unless you release my niece Emma from your evil power straight away, you're going to find yourself in more trouble than a pork pie at a Jewish wedding!

Witchfinder You dare to threaten me?! Why you great wobbly lump of jelly! I'll . . .

Dame Well go on Danny! Spell him!

Sir Daniel (*stepping forward*) Hold sirrah! I have something to say to you!

Witchfinder Well?

Sir Daniel (*incanting*) This magick spell commands stand fast ye!
                      Witchfinder General Grimnasty!

Grimnasty freezes in mid-scowl

Dame Blimey! It works! Right, ingredients. Have you got the virgin's hair?

Sir Daniel Er . ,. yes. It's here.

Dame (*interested*) Where d'you get it then?

Sir Daniel Never you mind.

Dame It looks like yours.

Sir Daniel It certainly isn't! (*Hastily*) Where's the frogspawn?

Dame (*rummaging in her handbag*) Here we are . . .

Sir Daniel (*gingerly taking the jar*) Now for the stolen kiss!

Dame Right! Emma, come here!

Emma (*stepping between them*) What's going on?!

Dame Dumpling grabs Emma and spins her around to face Sir Daniel, who plants a kiss on the end of her nose

(*Distantly*) What? How? Where am I? What's been happening?

Dame Quickly! (*Indicating Grimnasty*) Give him the kiss!

Sir Daniel I have to kiss HIM?!

Dame Well kiss me and I'll kiss him . . .

Sir Daniel I'd rather kiss a warthog!

Dame Well he's a bit of a bore, kiss him!

Sir Daniel (*kissing Grimnasty*) Right! Kiss . . . hair . . .
                      By stolen kiss and frogspawn load,

And virgin's hair—become a toad!!!
Here goes with the frogspawn ...

As he goes to throw the frogspawn over Grimnasty, Smallpiece rushes on and interposes himself

Smallpiece No, no! Master! Watch out!

The frogspawn is deposited on Smallpiece. There is a flash and a bang, followed by a Black-out, during which Smallpiece exits

When the Lights come back up and the smoke clears, Smallpiece has gone!

Witchfinder (*snapping out of it*) What?! What's going on?! Aaaaargh! Witchcraft! Where's Smallpiece? (*He notices a small shape on the ground*) Smallpiece?

Smallpiece's voice Rivet?

Witchfinder (*apoplectically*) Madam! You have turned my assistant into a toad!

Dame 'Bout time he towed the line. Toad the line!! Geddit?!! (*To the audience*) Oh forget it ...

Witchfinder (*warming to his theme*) But your diabolical attempt to thwart me has failed! And now, you shall pay the penalty! Ha ha ha ha!!! (*To Emma*) Guard these dogs well! I shall prepare the instruments of execution!

He exits

Dame Oh no! Now we've blown it!

Emma Wait a moment! Will someone please explain what's going on?! What does he mean? Why does he think I should guard you?

Sir Daniel You were under his evil spell for a while, my love. But no longer. I released you with a kiss!

Emma Oh Daniel!

Sir Daniel Oh Emma!

Dame Oh no! There's no time for that! Come on, we've got to think fast!

Smallpiece's voice Rivet?

Dame (*stamping on him*) And you can shut up!

Emma (*picking up the squashed object*) Oh Auntie!

Dame Well, never did like toads. Nasty, slimy things! Particularly toads sporting little sniffers!

Sir Daniel What are we going to do now?

Dame We need another spell ...

Sir Daniel Yes, but where can we get one?

Dame I don't know! Who do you think I am? CEEFAX?

Sir Daniel You mean ORACLE.

Dame That's what I said!

Emma (*quietly*) I could do one of my spells ...

Dame (*patronizingly*) Yes dear, of course you could. (*Double-take*) One of yours?!!!! You can do spells?!

Emma Yes. Well, a few anyway ...

Sir Daniel But, that means you must be ...
Emma Yes, I am a witch!

Thunder, lightning, and atmospheric effects! Emma is illuminated in a blazing shaft of light. She seems to grow in stature, then as the Lights return to normal she appears her old self again

Dame You never told me! Oooh! Fancy that! A witch in the family!
Sir Daniel But how can you be a witch? You're not old and ugly! (*He gestures towards Dame Dumplings*) She is! But you're not!
Emma I have been secretly training to be a white witch. Working spells to help people.
Dame Well I hope you've got a spell to help us, my little pudding, otherwise we'll all end up on the barbecue. Witches or not!
Emma I think I might have an appropriate spell ... but I'll need some ingredients.
Sir Daniel What do you need?
Emma Well, first of all, a pair of pink knickers.
Sir Daniel Dame Dumplings?
Dame Oh no! Certainly not! Not in front of all these people!
Sir Daniel (*sternly*) It is your duty! Think of England!
Dame I'm thinking of the audience mate! They might not have eaten yet!
This magick spell commands—stand fast ye!
Dame Oh flamin' heck! Here you are then ... (*She lifts her skirts to reveal capacious pink undergarments, which she removes with some difficulty, and to undoubted audience participation, whistling etc.!*)
Sir Daniel Right! What else?
Emma Dear me. This is awkward. I need a hairy bottom ...

They both look expectantly at Dame Dumplings

Dame (*looking from one to the other in horror*) NO! Absolutely not! I'd rather be burnt! Anyway ... It isn't hairy, just a bit fluffy, that's all.
Emma Then we're finished. The spell will only work with a hairy bottom ...
Sir Daniel Where on earth can we get a hairy bottom?

Audience participation

What? No, no. Not a bare bottom, a hairy one ...
Emma (*Excitedly*) No! That's it! They mean Bottom the dancing bear!
Sir Daniel Yes! Of course! A hairy Bottom!
Dame Yes, but he's not here is he?!

Peter Farthing wanders on

Peter Has anyone seen my Bottom?
Dame Just what we were thinking! Where did you spring from?
Peter We were supposed to be entertaining the garrison, but my assistant, the lovely Bottom, has done a bunk again! They're trying to catch him now!

Nathaniel and Obadiah chase Bottom on through the audience

Nathaniel Oi! Come here! We want a word with you, sir! Fur coats is against regulations!

All Bottom!

Bottom makes it on to the stage, closely followed by Nathaniel and Obadiah. All collapse in a gasping heap on the floor

Dame There you are. One hairy Bottom, complete with a couple of pimples!

Emma (*sweetly*) Peter, may we borrow your bear for a few moments?

Peter (*puzzled*) Of course ...

The Witchfinder enters

Witchfinder Aha! More miscreants eh?! Never mind! Plenty of room on the bonfire! Ha ha ha!

Audience participation

Emma (*urgently*) Nicholas, I must tell you something!

Witchfinder Well?

Emma (*incanting*)   This magick spell commands—stand fast ye!
                          Witchfinder General Grimnasty!

Dame Ha! He's under again! Well go on then, Mr Majeika. (*Or other topical magician*) Get on with it!

Emma   By knickers pink, and Bottom hairy,
                          You shall be changed—into a fairy!!!

She throws the underwear at him, and pushes Bottom towards him. The knickers land on Grimnasty's hat, and the bear enbraces him. There is a huge flash, bang and Black-out. When the smoke clears, Grimnasty is revealed in the regalia of a Christmas Fairy, including silver frock, tinsel crown, wand and glitter. Bottom—who is still embracing him—yelps and backs away

Witchfinder Well? What are you lot staring at?! (*He looks down at himself*) Aaaaargh!

Dame Blimey! it's Tinker Bell!

Emma (*surprised*) It worked!

Witchfinder (*faintly*) I've come across a little queer ...

Dame (*moving away*) So have I mate ...

Witchfinder How dare you! What have you done? I command you to change me back again!

Dame What are you going to do? Hit us with your handbag?

Emma I'm sorry. I don't know the reversal spell. It can't be done.

Witchfinder What do you mean "can't be done"?

Dame Can't be done.

Witchfinder (*brokenly*) Then I am undone ...

Peter Indeed you are. For now, you are part of Christmas itself: the Christmas Fairy! Compelled to spend the rest of your days sitting on top of the Christmas Tree!

Dame (*maliciously*) Yes! And you know where the pointed bit goes, don't you?!

Obadiah Hey! This means no more gloom! No more misery!

Dame Then Christmas can go ahead as usual!

Peter And so can the party!

All HOORAY!!!

Emma (*taking Sir Daniel's hand*) And we can take up where we left off . . .

Sir Daniel Oh Emma!

Emma Oh Daniel!

Dame (*giving up*) Oh ruddy hell!

Nathaniel Here! All this romantic stuff is against regulations, you know!

Dame Oh don't be such a spoilsport! If you can't beat 'em, join 'em! You know what you need, Natty?

Nathaniel (*warily*) What?

Dame (*leaping into his arms*) A generous portion of Dumplings!!!

Nathaniel (*staggering under the weight*) Now I'm really in a stew!

Music, as the village children enter

Peter	And so our tale comes to a close,
	We hope you've all had fun,
	And that you all enjoy yourselves
	At Christmas, every one.
Sir Daniel	They tried to stop our Christmas fun,
	But we showed them what we meant!
Witchfinder	I started out to set them straight,
	But I've ended rather bent . . .
Emma	I've found my dashing cavalier,
Sir Daniel	And I my maiden fair.
Nathaniel	All I've got's a load of Dumplings.
Obadiah	I'd rather have the bear!
Dame	We hope your parties are all great fun,
	With lots of Christmas cheer,
	And now, we're going to the pub,
	To guzzle lots of beer!
	So, good-night and . . .

All MERRY CHRISTMAS!!!

Song (Entire cast)

CURTAIN

FURNITURE AND PROPERTY LIST

ACT I

SCENE 1

On stage: Large throne on dais
Macabre banners

Off stage: Halberds **(Nathaniel** and **Obadiah)**

SCENE 2

On stage: Snow-laden cottages, one with practical door
Broom behind door
Tree-stump

Off stage: Bags and bundles of wares including sweets **(Peter)**
Flowers **(Emma)**

Personal: **Dame:** coins
Sir Daniel: signet ring

SCENE 3

On stage: Sparse and gnarled trees

Off stage: Small twig **(2nd Crone)**
Large log **(Sir Daniel)**

SCENE 4

On stage: As Scene 2

Check: Broom behind door

Off stage: Notices, nails, hammer **(Nathaniel** and **Obadiah)**
Tray of hot mince pies **(Dame)**
Covered basket containing crackers, paper chains, mince pies **(Emma)**

Personal: **Obadiah:** handkerchief, sweets
Dame: sweets

ACT II

SCENE 1

On stage: Fiendish contraptions

Grisly remains
Stocks on raised block with chains for **Emma**
Thumbscrews
Bag of charcoal
Red-hot poker
Long feather for **Smallpiece**

Off stage: Large dusty volume with pictures **(Smallpiece)**

Personal: **Emma:** bright handkerchief tied round face
Witchfinder: shiny pendant

SCENE 2

On stage: As Act I, Scene 2

Personal: **Peter:** pristine handkerchief

SCENE 3

On stage: As Act I, Scene 2

No other props required

SCENE 4

On stage: Nil

Off stage: Bear's head from costume **(Sir Daniel)**

SCENE 5

On stage: As Act I, Scene 2

No other props required

SCENE 6

On stage: As Act I, Scene 2

Off stage: Mince pie **(Bottom)**

SCENE 7

On stage: Huge cauldron belching green smoke
Salt, spoon

Personal: **Sir Daniel:** silver coin
1st Witch: scrap of paper

SCENE 8

On stage: As Act I, Scene 1

During Black-out on page 34, set small toad on ground

Personal: **Sir Daniel:** lock of hair
Dame: handbag containing jar of frogspawn
Witchfinder: fairy outfit, wand, crown under cloak

LIGHTING PLOT

Property fittings required: nil

Various simple interior and exterior settings

ACT I, SCENE 1

To open: Dark, sinister lighting, flashes of lightning

No cues

ACT I, SCENE 2

To open: General exterior lighting

No cues

ACT I, SCENE 3

To open: Dim lighting, with eerie flickering lights

Cue 1   **2nd Crone:** "You may be surprised."   (Page 9)
         Dim lights further

ACT I, SCENE 4

To open: General exterior lighting

No cues

ACT II, SCENE 1

To open: Dim dungeon lighting, single shaft of light from high above
         Emma

Cue 2   **Witchfinder** hypnotizes **Emma** and **Smallpiece**   (Page 19)
         Fade to black-out

ACT II, SCENE 2

To open: General exterior lighting

No cues

ACT II, SCENE 3

To open: General exterior lighting

No cues

ACT II, SCENE 4
To open: Dark, gloomy lighting
No cues

ACT II, SCENE 5
To open: General exterior lighting
No cues

ACT II, SCENE 6
To open: General exterior lighting

Cue 3	**Peter:** "... thanks for all your help!" *Dim lights*	(Page 28)
Cue 4	**Peter** and **Bottom** exit *Dim lights further; lightning flashes*	(Page 28)

ACT II, SCENE 7
To open: Dim lighting, with eerie flickering lights
No cues

ACT II, SCENE 8
To open: Dark, sinister lighting

Cue 5	Frogspawn is deposited on **Smallpiece** *Black-out*	(Page 34)
Cue 6	When ready *Return to previous lighting*	(Page 34)
Cue 7	**Emma**: "Yes, I am a witch!" *Lightning; blazing shaft of light on **Emma** for a few moments, then return to previous lighting*	(Page 35)
Cue 8	**Emma** throws knickers at **Witchfinder** *Black-out*	(Page 36)
Cue 9	When ready *Return to previous lighting*	(Page 36)

EFFECTS PLOT

ACT I

Cue 1   As Scene 1 begins   (Page 1)
Thunder crashes mist

Cue 2   Boy taps on the door   (Page 3)
Crashing and banging

Cue 3   **Dame** "I'm just stuffing a tart!"   (Page 3)
Crashes

Cue 4   **Dame** chases children round in circles   (Page 4)
Bell rings, off

ACT II

Cue 5   As Scene 1 begins   (Page 17)
Distant gibbering screams, incessant dripping noise—gradually fade

Cue 6   As Scene 4 opens   (Page 23)
Wind

Cue 7   **Peter:** "... thanks for all your help!"   (Page 28)
Distant rumble of thunder

Cue 8   **Peter** and **Bottom** exit   (Page 28)
Thunder crashes, wind howls, driving rain

Cue 9   **Dame** and **Sir Daniel** exit   (Page 29)
Fade wind and rain; mist, thunder rolls ominously, wolf howls nearby, green smoke from cauldron

Cue 10   Frogspawn is deposited on **Smallpiece**   (Page 34)
Flash and bang

Cue 11   **Emma:** "Yes, I am a witch!"   (Page 35)
Thunder, atmospheric effects

Cue 12   **Emma** throws knickers at **Witchfinder**   (Page 36)
Huge flash and bang

MADE AND PRINTED IN GREAT BRITAIN BY
LATIMER TREND & COMPANY LTD PLYMOUTH

MADE IN ENGLAND